A Love Letter Unwritten

This isn't just a story — it's a real-life experience, a journey that felt truly magical for the first time in my life. This book is dedicated to the moments I've shared with you and the ones I've lived without you. It's a saga of our story, an attempt to immortalize the connection we shared. Even if we lose touch, this book will serve as a testament to our bond, a way to keep our story alive forever, capturing the essence of what we were and what we still are, deep within. Through these pages, I hope you'll always feel the emotions that once tied us together, no matter where life takes us.

This book expresses all my love for you, love that I probably failed to convey in words over the years. I know I wasn't the best at expressing my feelings directly. Instead, I poured my heart into the little things, quietly taking care of your needs, anticipating your thoughts, and trying to make sure you always felt special.

Every gesture, no matter how small, was my way of saying, "I love you." From remembering your favorite snack to staying up late just to wait for you to come home, I hoped my actions would speak the words I found hard to say. I watched over you, not out of obligation, but because your happiness became my happiness. Each time I made you smile, it felt like I was adding another beautiful chapter to our story.

But I also know that sometimes words are necessary, that sometimes you needed to hear those three simple words spoken aloud. I regret the times I held back, thinking my actions were enough. This book is my way of making up for that silence, of finally putting into words everything that has always been in my heart. I hope that as you turn these pages, you'll feel the depth of my love, the love that has always been there, even when I struggled to express it. This is my love letter to you, the one I never wrote, but always felt.

Index

Before You Came Along

The story begins a few years before I met you, with a young man who had been deeply hurt. His heart was broken, scarred by a first love that ended in lies and betrayal. The pain ran so deep that it left him questioning everything he once believed in. Love, once a dream, had turned into a nightmare he couldn't wake up from. Trust seemed like a distant memory, and the idea of commitment became something he feared rather than desired.

This man had grown up too fast. From a young age, he had shouldered the weight of his entire family's responsibilities. He became the pillar they leaned on, the one who always had to be strong, even when he felt like crumbling inside. Each day was a battle as he struggled to build a career, trying to earn enough to support those who depended on him. The pressure was immense, and the dreams he once had began to fade into the background as survival became his only focus.

In the midst of this turmoil, he built walls around his heart, believing that love was a luxury he could no longer afford. Life had taught him to be cautious, to guard his emotions, and to protect himself from the pain he knew all too well. He was lost in the demands of life, trudging through each day with the weight of his past dragging him down. Love seemed like a distant, unattainable concept—something meant for others, but not for him.

But life has a way of surprising us when we least expect it. Just when he thought his heart had been hardened beyond repair, you entered his life. Little did he know that meeting you would be the beginning of a new chapter, one that would rewrite everything he thought he knew about love and about himself. You were the light that began to shine through the cracks in his armor, gently reminding him that love could still exist, even in the most unexpected of places.

The Unexpected Encounter

I visited your city for some office work, never imagining that this trip would change my life. It was there, amidst the hustle and bustle, that I saw you for the first time. The moment our paths crossed, something inside me shifted. I don't know why, but I felt an inexplicable pull towards you, as if some invisible force was drawing me in. A strange, almost foolish smile spread across my face, one that I couldn't seem to wipe away. It was as if that smile had been pasted on, and nothing could erase it.

From that moment, I was captivated. I wanted to know you, to talk to you, to see more of you. My heart raced, my mind spun, and every inch of my body and soul seemed to cry out, urging me to be closer to you. Little did I know that this feeling would grow into something far deeper than I could have ever imagined, something I had never felt or experienced before.

As I went about my day, it was as if the universe itself was conspiring to bring us together. Everywhere I turned, I saw signs — subtle hints that seemed to point me back to you. It felt like the world was whispering in my ear, telling me that it was you and only you. I couldn't shake the feeling that something greater was at work, that our meeting was more than just a coincidence.

I was utterly mesmerized by that one encounter we had
at your workplace. Your presence left an indelible mark
on me, and I found myself replaying the moment over
and over in my mind. The way you moved, the way you
spoke — it all left me in awe. I knew, even then, that I
wanted more. I wanted to understand the person behind
that captivating exterior, to unravel the mystery that was
you. And as the days went on, the thought of you
lingered, growing stronger with each passing moment.

It was as if my heart had found something it had been
searching for all along, without even knowing it. Meeting
you was like discovering a missing piece of myself, a
piece I hadn't realized was lost. And from that day
forward, my life was never quite the same.

The Inner Struggle

I knew I was drawn to you, felt a magnetic pull that made me certain I wanted to be with you. But at the same time, my dark past was a relentless voice in my head, urging me to resist these feelings, to stop seeing you, and even to push away the thoughts of you. My life was already weighed down by responsibilities, and the idea of adding something new felt overwhelming. I was consumed by fears that I might not be able to take care of you the way you deserved, that I might fail to fulfill your needs and desires.

The thought of not being able to keep you happy was terrifying. I wrestled with the fear that I wouldn't be able to meet all your expectations or provide the support you needed. The idea of hurting you, even unintentionally, was too painful to bear. All I ever wanted was to be the person who could fulfill your needs, to offer you the love and care you deserved.

Caught in this storm of self-doubt and anxiety, I found myself taking a step back, overwhelmed by the weight of my worries. But then, amidst all this turmoil, a single conversation with you changed everything. That brief interaction was like a balm to my troubled mind, sweeping away the negativity and doubts that had clouded my thoughts. Your words, your presence, they brought back a sense of peace and joy that I hadn't felt in a long time.

In that moment, my fears seemed to dissolve, and that strange, silly smile returned to my face. It was as if your conversation had the power to erase all my challenges and scars, making everything seem possible again. You made me forget my struggles and reminded me of the happiness I had been missing. For the first time in a long while, I felt hopeful and reassured, knowing that despite my fears, there was something incredibly special and worth pursuing with you.

A Not-So-Perfect First Date

After a long wait and a few conversations with you, the day finally arrived when you planned to visit my city. I was beyond excited—like a child who sees their favorite person after a long time. Butterflies fluttered in my stomach, and I felt a mix of anticipation and nervousness. I wanted this meeting to be perfect, to make a lasting impression on you.

Although it wasn't a date, I treated it with the same care and attention. I meticulously planned every detail, ensuring that the meeting didn't resemble a typical date but still provided a memorable experience. I chose the best café in town, renowned for its exceptional food and coffee, and arranged for everything to be just right. I wanted to create an environment where we could talk comfortably and where you would feel special.

I spent almost two days preparing for our conversation, determined to have a meaningful and engaging discussion. I arrived at the café well before our meeting time, making sure you wouldn't have to wait. I selected the perfect table and briefed the café manager to ensure that everything ran smoothly. Even the manager could see the excitement in my eyes—he knew this was a significant moment for me.

But when you walked into the café, I was completely thrown off. The meticulous preparation I had done seemed to vanish in an instant. The moment I saw you, I lost my composure. Despite all my efforts to be poised and articulate, I found myself rambling, my words tumbling out in a disjointed stream. I forgot my carefully prepared script and the points I wanted to discuss.

As I blabbered on, I knew I was talking nonsense, my conversation lacking coherence and direction. I was jumping from one topic to another, my words failing to make the impact I had hoped for. I worried that instead of impressing you, I was making a mess of things. Yet, despite my rambling and disorganized chatter, you listened intently, your attention unwavering.

Your patience and interest made me realize that maybe, just maybe, it wasn't about being perfect. It was about the genuine connection we were building, the way you engaged with me despite my clumsiness. In that moment, I understood that being authentic was more important than any prepared speech. And as our conversation continued, I began to feel a sense of ease, comforted by your presence and the warmth of our shared moments.

Office Intrigue and Farewell Blues

After our café meeting, you planned to visit my office, and once again, I was as excited as a little kid. Everyone in the office knew about your visit; they had seen how your presence had filled me with an almost childlike joy. My colleagues were eager to meet the person who had me floating on cloud nine, and the anticipation in the air was palpable.

I remember vividly how you were in a cab, trying to find your way to my office, but the directions were a bit unclear. I was on the phone with you, anxiously trying to guide you, but I could sense the confusion in your voice. Worried that you might get lost, I rushed out of the office and ran down the street, scanning the busy traffic for your cab. The moment I spotted it, I didn't think twice—I dashed through the moving cars and jumped into your cab to make sure you got to my office safely. It was a reckless move, but in that moment, the excitement and adrenaline overrode any sense of caution. All I cared about was seeing you again.

As we walked into the office together, I could feel the eyes of my colleagues on us. They were staring, making it all too obvious, and I couldn't help but feel a little embarrassed. But at the same time, I was proud to have you there, to introduce you to the people I worked with every day. You met the team, and despite the awkwardness, everything felt right. You even managed to complete the counseling session you came for, but I couldn't help but notice the way my colleagues were looking at me afterward, teasing me relentlessly. I was blushing like a schoolboy, caught between embarrassment and happiness.

The next day, you had a flight to catch, and the thought of you leaving left me feeling a bit heartbroken. It was hard to accept that our time together was so short. Even though we continued our conversations over phone calls and texts, it wasn't quite the same as having you there in person. There was a quiet sadness in knowing that the moments we shared were fleeting, but at the same time, there was comfort in the connection we had built, a bond that seemed to grow stronger with each passing day.

Despite the distance, our conversations kept me going, filling the void your absence left behind. And though I was upset about you leaving, I found solace in the knowledge that this was just the beginning of something special, something worth holding onto no matter where life took us.

A New Visit, A New Beginning

Our conversations continued, and by now, it felt as if we were both being drawn to each other by some invisible force, as if the universe had been orchestrating this connection long before we even met. But as much as I cherished our phone calls, the reality of life began to weigh on me again. The struggles that had always been there—the mood swings, the bitterness, the self-doubt—started to creep back into my life, pulling me down into a familiar darkness. I felt a shift within me, one that only your presence could erase. I'm sure you sensed it too, even though I tried my best to hide it from you. But I wasn't good at hiding, and I'm sorry that you had to bear the brunt of my challenges.

Amidst all of this, you changed cities, but even then, you planned another visit just to see me, to spend some time together. I can't express how much that meant to me. This visit was special, and it was during this time that I first experienced your endearing clumsiness—when you forgot my gift at the airport. The whole situation was hilarious, and it made me fall for you even more. Meeting you again made all my troubles disappear, if only for a while. In those moments, nothing else mattered but seeing you, talking to you, and watching you smile.

It was during this visit that I realized just how deeply I had fallen for you. I couldn't stop myself from wanting to express my feelings, to let you know just how much you meant to me. Once again, I tried to plan everything out, determined to make this moment perfect. But as always, with you around, my preparations seemed to unravel. My heart was pounding so fast that I could hear it echoing in my ears, my nerves on edge as I prepared to propose to you.

And then, in the midst of it all, I finally found the courage to speak the words I had been holding back. As I looked into your eyes, I could barely keep my emotions in check. The words tumbled out, my voice shaking with a mixture of fear and hope. But before I could finish, you sealed my proposal with a kiss, and in that instant, I knew — this was it. All the doubts, the struggles, the fears — they faded away, replaced by a feeling of pure, unadulterated joy.

In that moment, everything felt right in the world. I realized that every twist and turn in our journey had led us to this point, and I wouldn't have changed a thing. Your kiss was more than just an answer — it was a promise, a beginning of something beautiful that I knew would last a lifetime.

The Birthday Trip

Our visits became a regular occurrence, and our time together felt more and more like a necessity rather than a luxury. Then, on your birthday, you asked me to visit your city—a request I couldn't possibly refuse. This trip marked my first-ever solo journey by plane, and although I was the sole breadwinner of my family with a limited income and countless struggles, I knew I had to be with you on your special day. I carefully calculated and planned every detail of your birthday, despite not knowing anyone in your city who could help me organize it better. But somehow, I managed to pull it off, and I made it to your city, determined to make your day unforgettable.

I remember bringing along your favorite lamp—a gift that wasn't easy to find, but I knew how much it would mean to you. When you saw it, your face lit up with pure joy. The way the lamp made you so happy was worth all the effort. We went out for dinner, enjoyed each other's company, and then spent time together at your place. I couldn't help but notice how small, little things like the lamp and the soft glow of lights in your home brought you such happiness. I found myself observing and memorizing every tiny detail about you—your likes, your dislikes, the way your eyes sparkled when something delighted you.

We spent three days together, but it felt like the time flew by in an instant. Each moment was precious, and when it was time for me to leave, I felt a bittersweet ache in my heart. As I boarded the plane back home, I realized something profound: it was you. You were my new beginning, the one who had brought light into my life, and I knew deep down that you would be with me until the end. Leaving your city felt like stepping away from a dream back into the harsh reality of my struggles, but this time, I carried a smile on my face. The thought of you, of us, gave me the strength to face whatever challenges awaited me back home.

As I flew back, I couldn't stop thinking about those three days. I knew then that you were more than just a fleeting chapter in my life—you were the one I wanted to write the rest of my story with. The love we shared had become my anchor, my source of joy and hope, and no matter how tough life got, I knew that as long as I had you, I could endure anything. The struggles waiting for me at home didn't seem so daunting anymore, because now I had a reason to keep going—a reason to believe that no matter how difficult things got, I was no longer facing them alone.

A New Beginning, A Tough Test

Amidst all the hustle and bustle of our meetings, I received a job offer in Mumbai. I thought that perhaps this move would be the fresh start I needed, a way to escape the constant challenges and chaos that had become a part of my daily life. Just as you had moved to another city, leaving behind your hometown, I believed that relocating to Mumbai would help me find focus and distance myself from the turmoil. The idea of starting anew in a different city was both exciting and nerve-wracking. This would be my first time living away from my family and friends, and while the prospect of independence thrilled me, the thought of being alone also filled me with anxiety.

The day of my departure finally arrived. I bid a bittersweet farewell to my family and friends, my heart heavy with the weight of leaving everything familiar behind. Arriving in Mumbai, I found myself thrust into an entirely new world. Settling into a new place with a flatmate, in a city where everything was unfamiliar, was far from easy. Suddenly, the responsibility of taking care of myself and managing an entire household fell squarely on my shoulders. It was overwhelming — someone who had always been lovingly cared for by his parents was now struggling to learn how to navigate life on his own.

The new job, the unfamiliar surroundings, and the demands of maintaining a home all at once felt like too much to handle. The loneliness of being away from everyone I knew only added to the pressure. Every day was a battle between trying to adjust to this new way of living and managing the stress of a demanding job. On top of that, I had to keep my family updated, knowing that they were worried and stressed about my well-being. In the midst of all this, I realized that I was failing to give you the time and attention you deserved. I could sense the strain it was causing in our relationship, and it pained me to know that my struggles were affecting you as well.

The distance, both physical and emotional, began to take its toll on us. I could feel the tension growing between us, and it wasn't easy to deal with. I hated that I was causing you stress, that I was unable to be there for you in the way that I wanted to be. Yet, despite all the challenges, I knew deep down that I had to find a way to make this work—not just for me, but for us. The thought of losing you was something I couldn't bear, and even though I was struggling, I was determined to find my footing in this new life, to overcome the hurdles, and to prove that our love could withstand even the toughest of times.

Moving to Mumbai was supposed to be a fresh start, but it became a test of my resilience and our relationship. It was a difficult journey, one that pushed me to my limits and forced me to confront my fears and insecurities. But through it all, the thought of you kept me going. I knew that if I could just hold on, if I could find my way through this storm, I would come out stronger on the other side, and so would we.

When Love Turns to Loss

Moving to a new city with a better-paying job, I thought life would finally ease up. I imagined the extra income would help me breathe a little easier, but it didn't take long for reality to hit hard. Within just a few months, I found myself struggling to manage two households on my revised pay scale — sending money back home to my parents while trying to cover my expenses in Mumbai. The pressure was immense, and it was clear that this move wasn't benefiting me the way I had hoped. But quitting was never an option; it never crossed my mind. My family needed me, not just financially but emotionally as well.

There were deeper issues within my family, personal conflicts that I had to mediate over long, draining phone calls. As the responsible son, it was my duty to keep the peace, to be the glue that held everything together. But the stress of it all was beginning to take its toll, not just on me but on us. I could feel the strain in our relationship, and it was tearing me apart. What hurt the most was knowing that it was affecting you more than anything. You were already far from your family, dealing with the ghosts of your past, and here I was, adding to your burden.

The weight of my responsibilities, combined with your own personal struggles, created an unbearable tension. And then, in a moment that I still struggle to comprehend, you took a drastic step — one that I could never have imagined, not even in my darkest nightmares. You attempted to take your own life. The news reached me like a bolt of lightning, shocking me to my core. It came from your flatmate, who called me late that night to relay the terrifying details. Her voice was a mix of accusation and concern, as if she was holding me responsible for pushing you to that brink. But I couldn't focus on her words; all I could think about was you.

Panic and helplessness gripped me. I wanted to drop everything and rush to your side, to be there for you, to make sure you were safe. But I had no idea where you were, no information about the hospital where you had been admitted. I felt utterly powerless. With just one common contact, I was left in the dark, grasping for any shred of information. Desperate, I sent messages to your friend every morning, afternoon, evening, and night, praying for some news, any sign that you were okay. But the responses were few and far between, and when they did come, they were cold and distant.

Each passing day was a torment. I was broken, consumed by fear and guilt. I couldn't sleep; nightmares haunted me, and I found myself crying, praying, pleading with the universe for your recovery. I was terrified that I might have been the final push, the last straw that drove you to such a desperate act. The thought that I might have caused you that much pain was unbearable, and in that moment, I made a decision that shattered my heart—I decided to step out of your life.

I thought that by removing myself, I could give you the space to heal, to rebuild your life without the added burden of my struggles. But that decision scarred me in ways I could never have anticipated. The memory of that night, the fear and helplessness, still haunts me to this day. Even now, I wake up in a cold sweat, my heart racing as I relive those moments in my mind. The nightmares refuse to fade, and every time I think of you, I'm overwhelmed with a deep sense of dread, wondering if you're okay, if you've found the peace and happiness you deserve.

This chapter of our story is one that I can never forget, no matter how hard I try. It changed me, reshaped my understanding of love, responsibility, and the fragility of life. And even though it's painful to revisit these memories, they remain a part of me, a testament to the depth of the emotions we shared and the impact you had on my life.

A Heart Torn in Two

The fear and anxiety were consuming me, making it impossible to focus on anything—work, life, even the simplest of tasks. My thoughts were fixated on you, constantly haunted by the uncertainty of your well-being. Every day, I scoured your social media profiles, searching for any sign of life, any indication that you were still out there, fighting, surviving. I needed to know that you had made it through, that you were okay. But the silence was deafening, and it only fueled the terror that gripped me tighter with each passing day.

Nearly a week passed in this agonizing limbo—seven days of sleepless nights, relentless anxiety, and a mind that wouldn't rest. Then, like a fragile lifeline thrown to a drowning man, I received a message from another friend of yours. She told me that you had survived, that you were recovering. The relief was overwhelming, a tidal wave of emotion that crashed over me. But even in that moment of solace, I knew. It had to be you who asked your friend to reach out, to let me know you were okay. That realization brought with it a profound and painful clarity: I had to make the hardest decision of my life.

Your life is precious, more precious than anything in this world, and to keep it safe, I knew I had to remove myself from it—even if it meant tearing my heart apart in the process. The thought of staying away from you, of never hearing your voice or seeing your smile again, was unbearable. But the thought of hurting you, of being the reason you might suffer again, was something I could not live with. I knew what I had to do, even if it killed me inside.

With a heavy heart, I made the decision to block you from all communication. I knew it would hurt you, and that knowledge tortured me. I imagined you recovering, trying to piece your life back together, only to find me gone—vanished without explanation. It was a cruel step, one that felt like a betrayal, but in my mind, it was the only way to protect you. I convinced myself that this pain, this loss, was temporary, and that eventually, you would heal. You would move on, stronger without me weighing you down.

But deep down, I knew I was being selfish. I was running away, not just from you but from the responsibility of my own emotions. The truth was, if I spoke to you, if I heard your voice even once, I would crumble. I would melt under the weight of my love for you, and I wouldn't have the strength to do what I believed was necessary. So, I did what I thought was best—I pushed you away, convinced that I was sparing you further pain. But in reality, I was only adding to it, all the while drowning in the guilt and self-blame for what you had gone through.

Every moment of every day, I replayed the events in my mind, wondering if I was the last push, the final straw that led you to that dark place. I blamed myself for your suffering, for the pain you endured. It was a burden I carried with me, a scar that would never fully heal. And as much as I tried to convince myself that I was doing the right thing, the emptiness inside me grew, a hollow ache that nothing could fill.

In the end, I had made a choice—a choice that tore us apart, but one I hoped would keep you safe. Even if it meant losing you forever, even if it meant living with the pain of that decision for the rest of my life, I knew I would do it again. Because your happiness, your safety, meant more to me than anything else. Even more than my own survival.

Fragile Echoes

I knew you were surrounded by people who loved you — your family, your friends — people who could offer the support and comfort I couldn't from afar. You were in a safe zone, where you could find solace and, perhaps, begin to heal. I convinced myself that my disappearance would allow you to move on, that those around you would help you forget the pain I had unintentionally caused. But while you were in the embrace of your loved ones, I was left alone, wrestling with thoughts darker than the abyss itself.

Every day felt like a battle against the overwhelming urge to reach out. I longed to hear your voice, just once, to know you were truly okay. I wanted nothing more than to rush to your side, to hold you close, to promise you that I would shield you from every hurt, that I would guard you with everything I had. But I had already taken that irreversible step — I had blocked you from all contact. I had severed our connection in the name of protecting you, and I was trapped in the torment of that decision.

Then, one day, my phone rang. An unknown number flashed on the screen, and I hesitated, my heart pounding in my chest. I answered, and there it was — your voice, soft but unmistakable. Tears welled up in my eyes, and I felt a surge of relief so intense it nearly brought me to my knees. I could barely speak, my throat tight with emotion, but I managed to ask, "How are you?"

You told me you were fine, recovering slowly, and with a quiet strength, you asked me to unblock you. My heart twisted inside my chest. I knew I shouldn't, that I should stand by my decision to keep my distance. But how could I deny your request? How could I say no when all I wanted was to hear your voice again and again? Against my better judgment, I agreed, and in an instant, we were back to our regular communication.

But things were different now. I spoke to you every day, yet something inside me had changed. I was more worried, more guarded. I felt a deep responsibility for your well-being, a weight I carried in silence. I wanted to ask you so many things — to understand what had driven you to such a drastic decision, to piece together the puzzle of your pain. But I held back, fearing that my questions might force you to relive that dark moment, might reopen a wound that was barely beginning to heal.

With your actions, something inside me died too. I became quieter, more cautious. My words, once so full of love and laughter, now felt like fragile things that could break us with the slightest misstep. I learned to swallow my thoughts, to bury my feelings deep within, fearing that anything I said might hurt you or push you away again.

Yet, every moment of silence was torture. I wanted to scream out my fears, my regrets, my undying love, but I stayed silent, trapped in a prison of my own making. I was torn between the need to protect you and the desperate desire to be close to you, to let you know that I was still here, still fighting for us — even if it meant battling against myself.

But as we spoke, day after day, I sensed a change in you too. There was something in your voice, something I couldn't quite place. Were you healing, or were you still broken beneath the surface? I wanted to know, needed to know — but I couldn't bring myself to ask. I was terrified of the answer. The suspense of it all was slowly tearing me apart, and yet, I clung to the hope that maybe, just maybe, we could find our way back to each other through the darkness.

I knew I had to tread carefully, that every word, every silence could tip the fragile balance. And so, I waited, holding my breath, hoping for a sign that we could still find our way back to the love we once shared. But the fear of losing you again loomed over me like a shadow, and I wondered if I would ever find the courage to tell you how much you still meant to me, or if I would remain locked in my own silence, forever caught in the tension between love and fear.

A New Beginning

As time passed, the silence within me grew, becoming an integral part of who I was. It was my refuge, my shield against the world. Confrontations, arguments—things I once might have faced head-on—became battles I fought silently, within the confines of my own mind. Disturbances, worries, frustrations—all of them were swallowed by the quiet, hidden away where no one could see. Silence became my healer, a balm for wounds that words could only deepen.

Our conversations were brief, yet meaningful, each one a small thread that wove us closer together. Every day, I watched as you grew stronger, your voice more vibrant, your spirit more resilient. The transformation was slow, but undeniable. Seeing you heal gave me hope—a fragile, delicate hope that maybe, just maybe, we could find our way back to each other. That maybe, we could be together again.

Then, one day, you called with unexpected news: you
had received a job offer in Mumbai. The thought of you
moving to the same city, of having you close again,
stirred something deep inside me. It was a mix of
excitement and anxiety, a fluttering in my chest that I
hadn't felt in a long time. You asked me where you
would stay if you moved to Mumbai, and though I was
already sharing my flat with a colleague, I didn't hesitate.
"Stay with me," I offered, knowing that having you
nearby, even temporarily, would mean the world to me.

The day of your arrival finally came. I could hardly
contain my excitement as I made my way to the airport,
my heart racing with anticipation. But I wasn't alone. My
colleagues, who had become like a second family to me,
were there too, eager to welcome you. As we waited, I
found myself lost in thought, wondering how it would
feel to see you again after everything we had been
through.

And then, there you were. The moment our eyes met, a
wave of emotion washed over me. You looked so much
healthier, stronger — a far cry from the fragile state you
had been in. Seeing you like that, standing there with
your suitcase and the lamp you had carried all the way
from home, filled me with a sense of relief and joy that I
hadn't felt in what seemed like an eternity.

We all greeted you with open arms, the warmth and love in the air palpable. It felt like a homecoming, not just for you, but for me as well. When we reached the flat, you settled into my room with ease, making yourself at home in the space that had once felt so empty without you.

For the first time in a long time, I felt at peace. Having you there, seeing you healthy and happy, was like a weight lifting off my shoulders. The silence that had once been my constant companion began to fade, replaced by the sound of your laughter, your voice filling the room. It was a new beginning, a second chance for us, and I was determined to make the most of it.

As we sat together that evening, surrounded by the familiar comforts of home, I couldn't help but smile. This was how it was meant to be — us, together, facing whatever the world threw at us, side by side. The future was uncertain, but for the first time in a long time, I felt hopeful. We had both been through so much, but now, with you by my side, I knew that we could overcome anything.

Moments of Bliss and Unspoken Battles

Having you around me made everything brighter, more colorful. I wanted the world to know how much you meant to me, so I brought you to my office, eager to introduce you to my colleagues. As I proudly introduced you to everyone, I could see the curiosity and excitement in their eyes. Many of them teased you playfully, making jokes about how you'd managed to win me over. It was all in good humor, but I could sense the discomfort behind your polite smiles. They adored me, and their teasing was meant to be lighthearted, but I knew it wasn't easy for you.

On the way home, I could feel the tension between us. You were quieter than usual, and I reached for your hand, gently squeezing it. I tried to reassure you, to explain that their jokes were just a reflection of how much they cared about me—and, by extension, you. With you, it was never hard to make peace. Your love for me was so pure, so unconditional, that you could never stay upset for long. You had this childlike innocence, a quality I cherished deeply. It made me want to do everything in my power to keep you happy, to see that radiant smile that could brighten even my darkest days.

I loved watching you—how you'd wrinkle your nose when you laughed, how you'd make silly faces just to make me smile. You were my joy, my reason to keep pushing forward, to keep striving to be better.

I had always been a fitness enthusiast, dedicated to my daily workouts and strict diet. But with you around, everything changed. Slowly, I started to skip my gym sessions. We found a new indulgence—ice cream. We would buy tubs of it and binge-watch movies late into the night, finishing the whole thing in one go. The nights stretched on like this, filled with laughter, movies, and far too many calories. I could see my body changing, my hard-earned muscles softening, but I didn't care. Every bite of ice cream, every skipped workout was a testament to how much I loved you, how deeply I was savoring every moment we spent together.

We began to explore the city together, going on small trips, creating new memories, and embarking on a house hunt for you. Your office was far from my flat, and the daily commute was starting to take its toll on you. I could see the exhaustion in your eyes each day as you returned home. I felt a pang of guilt every time I saw you struggling. It wasn't just the commute; it was also the fact that you were staying in my flat, a shared space with my colleagues, people I barely knew. I wanted you to have your own place, a sanctuary where you could feel completely comfortable and free, but I couldn't bring myself to say it. I feared my words would come out wrong or that you might misunderstand my intentions.

Months went by, and finally, we found a house that felt right. It was closer to your office, filled with light and positive energy. The moment you stepped inside, I saw your eyes light up with excitement. It was a space you could call your own, a place where you could arrange everything just the way you wanted. Watching you move into that new home, seeing the joy on your face as you unpacked and settled in, brought a strange mix of happiness and pain. I was glad you had found a place that felt like yours, but I also knew this meant that our days of living under the same roof had come to an end.

That first night after you moved out, I found myself lying awake in the quiet of my room. The silence was deafening. I missed the sound of your laughter, the way you'd steal the blankets in your sleep, the way the room felt warmer with you in it. I knew it was the right thing for you, but it didn't stop the ache in my chest. Our time living together had been so brief, just six months, but it had been filled with more life, more love, than I had ever known.

Seeing you thrive in your new space gave me comfort. You seemed happier, more at peace. And though I still felt the distance between us, I clung to the hope that this was just another chapter in our story, one that would lead to a deeper bond, a stronger connection. But there was a part of me that couldn't shake the feeling that we were standing on the edge of something uncertain, something fragile. I tried to push those thoughts away, to focus on the present, on the fact that you were still here, still with me.

Yet, in the quiet moments, I couldn't help but wonder if this was the beginning of something new or the start of an end I wasn't ready to face.

Small Moments, Grand Gestures

After you moved into your new place, our weekends became sacred. It was our time—just us. Sometimes, you'd come over and stay at my flat, filling the space with your presence, making everything feel lighter and more alive. Other times, I'd come over to your place, finding solace in the warmth you had filled it with, like it was a part of you, an extension of the love and comfort you carried in your heart.

I remember the first Valentine's Day we spent together. I had bought you a small gift, hoping to make you feel special in any way I could. When I handed it to you, you chuckled softly and teased me, saying that Valentine's Day was just for kids. You laughed at how earnestly I had approached it, but I didn't mind. I knew I was naive about these things, about what was expected or deemed "appropriate." I just wanted to show you how much you meant to me, in whatever way I could, even if it seemed silly. Your laughter in that moment, your eyes sparkling with amusement, were all the validation I needed.

Your sister came to visit soon after, and we decided to go on a short trip together. These little getaways became our rhythm, the pulse of our relationship. Before I met you, I never went on trips. I had always been cautious about my finances, counting every penny, always planning for a future that seemed so far away. But you… you showed me a different side of life. You introduced me to a world where experiences mattered more than money, where seeing new places and creating memories was an investment in its own right. With you, I began to discover the joy of exploration, the thrill of the unknown, and the beauty of living in the moment.

I started planning more carefully, saving up, investing with a future in mind — a future where I could take care of you, where we could build something secure and lasting together. Every choice I made from then on was with you in mind. The dreams I had were no longer just mine; they were ours.

Our birthdays were like no other — celebrations that seemed to stretch on for days. We made sure each one was unforgettable, filled with surprises, and more gifts than either of us could count. We would go out to party until the sun came up, or stay in, binge-watching movies, eating junk food, and making jokes about anything and everything. Some days we'd be out traveling, meeting new people, and seeing new sights; other days, we'd just enjoy each other's company, wrapped in the simplicity of being together. The days seemed brighter, the nights longer, filled with laughter and joy.

But it wasn't always easy. Behind the perfect moments, there were unspoken fears and insecurities. I wondered if I could ever really give you the life you deserved, if I was enough. I worried about whether you were truly happy or if I was just filling a void for you. But when I saw the way your eyes lit up when you looked at me, when you laughed at my silly jokes or held my hand in yours, those fears seemed to fade away.

Life felt perfect, almost too perfect, like a fragile glass that could shatter at any moment. We were building something beautiful, something meaningful. But deep inside, I knew that every great story has its trials, and every perfect moment is only a breath away from being tested. I tried not to dwell on those thoughts, choosing instead to focus on the love we had, the memories we were creating, and the future we were building.

But sometimes, in the quiet of the night, I wondered… how long could this perfection last? Was it real, or were we just holding onto a dream that could slip away at any moment?

A World Within Four Walls

When you moved out of your old home and settled close to mine, it felt like we had opened a new chapter in our story. Suddenly, we weren't just weekend companions. We were practically neighbors, and every day became an opportunity to see each other, to share moments, and to make new memories. This new house felt like it was built just for us—no flatmates, no interruptions, just you and me. Together, we set about decorating it, making it feel like ours, a sanctuary amidst the chaos of the world outside.

And then, the world changed. The pandemic struck, and everyone was confined to their homes. Fear and uncertainty filled the air, but for us, it became an unexpected blessing. You moved in with me, and even though my flatmates were there too, it felt like the universe had given us a chance to cocoon ourselves in this small world, just the two of us. Where others were desperate to step outside, I felt a strange sense of peace, content to be locked inside with you.

The days blurred together in a rhythm we created. I turned our small kitchen into a makeshift lab, experimenting with desserts, trying out recipes I'd never dared before. There was something magical about watching you smile as I presented my latest creation, the childlike glee in your eyes that made every effort worthwhile. Every meal became an event, a ritual. You insisted that I feed you, like a child craving comfort, and I indulged you, tearing pieces of food with my hand and bringing them to your lips. You'd say "nom nom" in that silly, sweet way, and I'd feel my heart swell with affection.

You always called me "Nana," a nickname that seemed to carry a universe of emotions within it. Sometimes, I'd wonder when you first started using it—was it from the very first day, or had it slipped in somewhere along the way, like a secret only we shared? We had so many names for each other, each one a little ridiculous, yet so filled with love—"Paagal Aadmi," "Paagal Aurat," "Kulta," "Ghople." These names were like our own language, a collection of sounds that could make us laugh or smile no matter what was happening around us.

But "Nana"—that one was special. Even now, the word rings in my ears, a sweet reminder of how you loved to tease me. You'd go out of your way to annoy me, just to see my exaggerated grumpy face, and then, with a sly grin, you'd shower me with your "Gold Fishy Kisses." I pretended to hate it, but truthfully, I lived for those moments, for that playful dance between us.

Every night, we fell asleep in each other's arms, a ritual that became as natural as breathing. I'd gently rub your forehead, stroking your hair until you drifted into sleep. These moments felt sacred, like a spell woven in the dark, binding us closer than ever. I wondered if we could ever be this close again, once the lockdown ended and life returned to its relentless pace.

In those months, I saw sides of you I hadn't known before — your vulnerability, your strength, your stubbornness, and your infinite capacity for love. We faced so much together, yet every challenge seemed to make us stronger. I realized then, as the world outside grew darker, our little universe was brighter than ever.

But in the back of my mind, a question lingered — how long could we keep this going? Could we hold onto this closeness, this happiness, once the world reopened and routine swept us back into its current? Was this time a gift, or was it setting us up for a future filled with inevitable change?

For now, I pushed those thoughts aside. I had you with me, and that was all that mattered. I held on to every "Nana," every "Gold Fishy Kiss," and every little moment in between, praying they would be enough to keep us strong in whatever came next.

Building Our Haven

The lockdown lifted, and with it came a new possibility —
a dream we'd both nurtured but had never spoken out
loud until now. We decided it was time to move in
together, to have a place that was truly ours. No more
shuffling between your flat or mine. We craved a home
where we could wake up and fall asleep under the same
roof, every single day.

We searched for weeks, combing through countless
listings, visiting one flat after another. But nothing felt
quite right until we found that one place — your favorite
society. The one you had admired for years, dreaming of
living there someday. It was an empty flat, a blank
canvas just waiting for us. The moment we stepped
inside, I saw the excitement in your eyes. This was the
one.

We moved in piece by piece, taking our time to make it
our own. I was genuinely surprised by your flair for
decorating; you were like an artist with a brush, painting
our future one detail at a time. You were far better than
any interior designer could have been. Every corner,
every nook of the flat had your touch — carefully chosen
furniture, soft lights that bathed the room in warmth,
vibrant plants that breathed life into our space, and
kitchen crockeries that seemed to reflect our shared love
for cooking and experimenting.

We invested not just money but also a lot of love, sweat, and laughter into this place. In a few short months, it transformed into a home—a sanctuary where I felt a sense of safety and comfort I had never known before.

Soon, the word spread. Your friends and my colleagues began visiting, and our weekends became filled with laughter and chatter. We hosted house parties where everyone stayed back, cherishing the view from our balcony, soaking in the effort and love we had put into every corner. I loved watching you play the perfect host, your eyes lighting up with pride as you showed off our creation.

Every day, I looked forward to coming home to you. We'd watch movies or binge on our favorite series, sharing meals we'd either cooked together or ordered in on lazy evenings. We found our rhythm in the everyday tasks—dividing chores, making sure neither of us felt overburdened. Even the mundane felt special when done together.

I found myself making excuses to skip office parties or outings with friends; nothing seemed more appealing than those quiet, intimate moments with you. You were my home. The thought of coming back to you was all I needed to get through the day. Your presence was my comfort, my sanctuary.

I loved how you'd dance around the living room or sing
with that slightly off-key but adorable voice, pulling me
into your silly antics until I couldn't help but join in.
Every day felt like a new adventure, filled with joy and
laughter. I'd walk in the door, and you'd always find a
way to hide, waiting for me to catch you in our little
game of hide and seek. When I did, we'd share a tight,
squeezing hug that felt like coming up for air after being
underwater.

I can still feel the softness of your cheeks beneath my
hands, the way I'd squeeze them, claiming them as my
perfect stress busters. Those moments became our daily
rituals, small but meaningful, building blocks of our love.

Yet, beneath all the joy, there was always a quiet question
in my mind — what if this was too good to be true? Could
something this perfect, this beautiful, really last? We were
building something fragile, like a house of cards, and I
held my breath, hoping it wouldn't come crashing down.

But every day, you reassured me with your laughter,
your love, and the way you made me feel like I was
exactly where I needed to be. For now, that was enough.
We had built our haven, and I was determined to protect
it with everything I had.

The Art of Surprises

After moving in together, my life took on a new rhythm, one where every beat was synchronized with thoughts of you. I found myself planning and dreaming more vividly than I ever had. Your birthday became the centerpiece of my calendar, a day I wanted to make unforgettable, every single year. I would start planning months in advance, meticulously noting down every detail—your likes, dislikes, your passing whims, and those fleeting moments of joy that I'd caught in your eyes.

I became a quiet observer, capturing every nuance of our time together, storing up little secrets in my mind. I wanted to ensure each birthday was not just special but magical. I wanted you to feel celebrated, cherished, and adored. Your friends became my co-conspirators. I'd reach out to them, gathering ideas and intel, trying to paint a picture of your perfect day. Slowly, piece by piece, the plan would come together.

I would start saving weeks ahead, putting aside every spare bit, so I could make it grand—bigger and better than the last one. I would choose the venue with care, a place that I knew would make your heart sing. I'd select the guest list with precision, inviting all the people who mattered to you, who brought you joy. I would pick the cake after countless tastings, wanting it to be just right. And the gift—it had to be perfect, something meaningful, something that spoke directly to your soul.

Every time I managed to surprise you, it felt like a small victory. The look of pure joy on your face when you walked into a room filled with everyone you loved made every sleepless night, every little worry, every penny saved completely worth it. I watched as you laughed and danced, surrounded by your friends, your happiness lighting up the room. Each year, the challenge became more thrilling—how could I top the last one? How could I make this next birthday even more special?

Your friends would often tell me they were amazed at the lengths I'd go to, how I managed to outdo myself year after year. I could see it in their eyes—they were impressed, even envious. But none of that mattered as much as your smile, the way your eyes would light up, the surprise that never faded from your face.

In truth, I think your birthday excited me more than it did you. I became a child again, caught up in the joy of creating something magical for the person I loved most. I poured over every detail—the theme, the music, the people, the food, the after-party snacks. Every choice, every decision was made with you in mind, to see that spark of happiness, to make you feel loved in a way words never could.

But there was always an undercurrent of suspense for me — a mix of anxiety and anticipation. Would I be able to surprise you yet again? Would this be the birthday that was remembered as our best? Or was I setting myself up for the year when I might fail to live up to your expectations?

Yet, every year, when that day arrived, I would see your smile, hear your laughter, and know that somehow, I had managed to make you feel special once again. And for me, that was enough. Each celebration became a new chapter in our story, another layer of memories that bound us together, making the love we shared even more profound.

The Unseen Void

The last birthday was meant to be the grandest of all — a celebration that would outshine every previous one. I had planned it with your friends, orchestrated every detail with the precision of a maestro, hiding every secret with the thrill of anticipation. I meticulously selected the venue, the food, and the cake, ensuring everything was perfect. But this year, there was a gap in my planning: a missing gift.

You never cared much for material things, and the grand surprise party was, in itself, a testament to how well I knew you. Yet, as the festivities unfolded, I couldn't shake the feeling that something was amiss. Despite the grandeur and the joy that filled the room, I noticed a shadow behind your laughter, a flicker of sadness in your eyes. You wore your child-like smile as usual, but it seemed to mask an underlying melancholy that I couldn't ignore.

It was disturbing, seeing you like this. My instinct was to probe, to ask, but the same anxiety that had plagued me in the past gripped me once more. I was caught in a storm of thoughts, wrestling with my own fears and uncertainties. I was fighting against the rising tide of self-blame, wondering if my own limitations were failing to bring you the happiness you deserved.

I could sense that something within you had shifted, an invisible weight that seemed to press upon your heart. It was as if the joy that once came so naturally was now overshadowed by an unspoken burden. It tore at me from within, the realization that despite my efforts, I couldn't reach you completely. I questioned my choices, my decisions, my ability to provide you with the future I had promised.

The fear of losing you loomed large, more menacing than ever before. It was as if the sands of time were slipping through my fingers, taking with them the happiness we had built together. The pressure to secure our future, to ensure that everything was stable and perfect, was becoming overwhelming. I felt trapped between the desire to fix what was wrong and the reality of my own limitations.

As the celebration continued, I forced myself to smile, to play the part of the perfect partner. But inside, I was a storm of emotions, struggling with the realization that no matter how grand the gesture, it couldn't always mask the void that seemed to grow between us. It was killing me to see you unhappy, even in the midst of everything that should have been perfect.

I needed to find a way to bridge this gap, to understand what was troubling you without risking further discord. But the fear of failing you, of not living up to the expectations I had set for myself, loomed large. I was in no position to take risks, to venture into unknown territories. All I could do was watch, helpless, as the shadow of uncertainty lingered over us.

The unspoken sadness became a haunting presence, a reminder that even the most meticulously planned surprises couldn't always fill the voids that lay beneath the surface. As I grappled with my own inadequacies, the future seemed to drift further from my grasp, leaving me in a state of profound turmoil.

The Silent Struggle

I was deeply saddened by the way you masked your sorrow, pretending that everything was fine when it was clear that something was troubling you. And like you, I too began to hide my own fears, concealing the nagging doubt that your sadness was somehow my fault. The question, "Was it because of me?" echoed relentlessly in my mind, and each time it did, a chill ran down my spine. Was I on the brink of losing you once again? The thought of separation, after all we had built together, was unbearable, shaking me to my core.

I found myself drowning in a sea of uncertainty, battling the relentless fear that perhaps my shortcomings were pushing you away. I needed to talk to someone—anyone—who could offer a shred of clarity. Before I could muster the courage to confront you directly, your friend reached out to me. Although I hadn't planned to confide in her, the dam broke during that unexpected call. In my desperation, I spilled everything, hoping she would keep it between us. For a brief moment, I felt a sense of relief, as if the weight on my chest had lightened. But the comfort was fleeting, quickly replaced by the gnawing dread that my worst fears could come true.

The possibility of losing you was destroying me from the inside out. I needed help—professional help—someone who could offer guidance and help me navigate this storm. I decided to see a therapist, a counselor who might help me unravel the tangled web of thoughts that had taken over my mind. I didn't know who else to turn to, and the idea of discussing my deepest fears with a stranger was daunting, but necessary.

Week after week, session after session, I laid bare the turmoil inside me. I described the heaviness in my heart, the sleepless nights filled with questions that had no answers. I sought advice on how to keep us together, how to bridge the growing distance between us, and how to protect what we had fought so hard to build. I wanted to understand where I was going wrong, what I could do to bring back the light in your eyes that I so dearly missed.

But each session was a double-edged sword. While it provided a temporary solace, it also forced me to confront my own inadequacies and fears. I wasn't just fighting for you—I was fighting for us, for the life we had envisioned together. My therapist offered insights and coping strategies, but the uncertainty lingered, a persistent shadow that haunted me even in my quietest moments.

Every day felt like walking on eggshells, trying to keep the peace without pushing too hard. I was terrified of making a wrong move, of saying something that might drive you further away. The stakes were high, and I felt ill-equipped to deal with the magnitude of what was at risk. The thought of separation was like a looming storm cloud, threatening to unleash chaos on everything we had built. I wasn't ready to face that possibility. I wasn't ready to lose you. But as the days passed, I knew I couldn't keep fighting this battle alone.

The silent struggle continued, each day a delicate balance of hope and fear, love and doubt. I was desperate for answers, for some sign that things would be okay. But in the absence of certainty, all I could do was hold on and hope that somehow, some way, we would find our way back to each other.

The Misstep

Diwali was approaching, and as always, I looked forward to the warmth of home, surrounded by family and friends in my hometown. It was a tradition I cherished, a time when everything seemed to slow down, allowing me to soak in the familiar comfort of loved ones and childhood memories. But this year, my heart was torn. You had your plans—a two-day outing with your friends that I secretly wished to be a part of. As much as I wanted to be with my family, the thought of being away from you gnawed at me.

In the past, whenever I traveled to my hometown, I often became so engrossed in the everyday rhythm of home that I would miss our daily conversations. Those lapses, those moments of silence, used to upset you. I remember how you would quietly express your disappointment, and over time, I learned to make it a priority to reach out, to call you every day. This time was no different; I called you every day, keeping our connection alive even from miles away.

I would check in on you often, especially when you were out late or traveling. I couldn't rest until I knew you were safe at home. I remember the quiet panic that would settle in when your phone was unreachable, or when a call went unanswered. It wasn't about control; it was the anxiety of not knowing if you were okay. I cared deeply, perhaps too deeply, and sometimes that care would spill over into fear. I even reached out to your friends when I couldn't reach you directly, just to make sure everything was alright.

But this time, during your two-day trip, something felt off. My calls went unanswered — not because of poor reception or missed notifications, but by choice. I sensed it immediately. When we finally spoke, there was a hesitance in your voice, a guardedness that I hadn't heard before. It didn't take long for me to piece it together: your friend, the one I had confided in during a moment of weakness, had shared everything with you. She had spilled every secret, every worry I had laid bare, believing she would keep it to herself. But more than that, it was the way she had told you — her version of events that was not only incomplete but altered in ways that twisted the truth.

I felt my world tilt. The realization hit me like a cold wave, washing over every ounce of relief I had briefly felt in confiding in her. It was too late. Whatever explanation I could muster wouldn't suffice, not now. The words that had come from a third party, however distorted, were the ones you believed. And in the tangled mess of misunderstandings, I was left grappling with the fallout.

I replayed every conversation in my head, cursing myself for trusting the wrong person. I should have spoken to you directly, should have laid it all out in front of you instead of seeking solace in someone else. But at that moment, when I was at my weakest, I had made a choice—a choice that now felt like a betrayal of everything we had built. I realized my error in judgment, a mistake that had opened a rift between us that I wasn't sure how to mend.

With the distance between us, separated by miles and the walls of our own emotions, I struggled to find a way to explain. How could I express the truth when every word felt inadequate, every sentence like a threadbare attempt to patch the widening gap? I had never been good with words; I had always shown my love through actions—small gestures, quiet comforts. But now, it seemed, actions alone were not enough.

As I sat in my childhood home, surrounded by the familiar sounds of Diwali, the laughter of family, and the crackle of fireworks outside, I felt a profound emptiness. The festival of lights, meant to chase away the darkness, only seemed to highlight the shadows that loomed over us. I feared that the light we once shared was dimming, and the thought of losing you terrified me.

I wanted to reach out, to bridge the distance that had grown between us, but the fear of making things worse held me back. And so, I sat with my thoughts, my regrets, and the nagging ache of uncertainty, hoping that somehow, someway, we could find our way back to each other before it was too late.

The Journey Back

Returning to you was always the highlight of my trips home. I couldn't wait to share all the stories of my parents, who you affectionately referred to as "Mumble" for my father and "Dhenti" for my mother. It was one of the many quirks that made us us. We had this pact—a simple rule to never drop each other off at the airport. Instead, we promised to always be there to welcome each other back. In our entire decade together, we never broke that promise. Every time I returned to Mumbai, you would be waiting for me at the airport, scanning the crowd for my tall frame. And every time you flew back from your trips, I would be there too, eager to spot you among the arriving passengers.

Sometimes, I'd try to surprise you, hiding in plain sight until your eyes, always searching, would finally find me. Your hugs were more than just greetings—they were my sanctuary. Every embrace felt like coming home, a tight, reassuring grip that said, "You are safe, you are loved." Those moments were my anchor, the reason I never feared stepping out into the world, because I knew I had you to come back to.

But this time was different.

This time, you weren't there.

As I stepped off the plane, scanning the sea of unfamiliar faces, your absence felt like a punch to the gut. The airport, once a place of joy and reunion, now felt cold and alien. My heart sank, my throat tightened. I tried to reassure myself — telling myself that you were waiting at home, that we'd talk things through, that we'd find our way back to each other. But a gnawing fear gripped me. What if the conversation with your friend had changed everything? What if this was the beginning of the end?

The drive home felt endless, each mile stretching into an eternity. My heart pounded with every passing second, my mind racing through a thousand scenarios of what awaited me. Would you be waiting with open arms, ready to mend the cracks? Or would you be distant, already having made up your mind about us? I stared out of the taxi window, watching the city blur past, each familiar landmark suddenly feeling foreign and unwelcoming.

I arrived at our building, the place that once felt like a warm, comforting cocoon. But now, the walls felt imposing, the elevator ride up unbearably slow. With every floor I ascended, my anxiety grew. I could barely breathe as I fumbled with my keys, each click of the lock echoing louder than my heartbeat. I opened the door, bracing myself for what I might find, every step towards our shared space heavy with uncertainty.

Would you be there waiting, ready to talk? Or would you have already decided it was time to let go? The suspense was suffocating, every second a struggle to keep myself composed as I stepped into what had always been our sanctuary, now feeling like the edge of an unknown abyss.

The Unraveling

On the way back from the airport, my mind was a storm of confusion and dread. Every time I thought of calling you, my fingers froze, paralyzed by the fear of what I might hear on the other end. I couldn't summon the courage to dial your number, to ask if everything was okay when I knew it probably wasn't.

When I finally stepped into our home, it felt emptier than ever before. You were still at work. I unpacked my bags, each item feeling heavier than usual, the silence of our apartment pressing down on me. I sat there, waiting, my heart a tangled mess of hope and fear. The minutes dragged, each one stretching like a cruel eternity until I heard the familiar jingle of keys at the door.

You walked in, and for a fleeting moment, everything felt normal. But then I saw your face — the forced smile that didn't reach your eyes, the sadness you tried so hard to hide. You greeted me warmly, as if nothing had changed, but I could sense the weight of what was left unsaid. I told you to freshen up first, buying myself a few more moments of quiet before the storm.

My heart pounded violently in my chest, each beat a
deafening reminder of the impending conversation. I
knew deep down that this was it. The end of us. The
realization was suffocating, but I kept my face as calm as
I could, masking the panic that clawed at my insides.
When you finally sat down, the room fell silent. The
tension between us was thick, almost tangible, and I
braced myself for the words that would change
everything.

You said you wanted to move out.

The words hung in the air, heavy and unyielding. You
had already made arrangements, spoke to your office,
and planned your transfer to another city — far from me,
far from everything we'd built together. You explained it
was for the best, that staying in the same place would
only hurt us more. You had a plan, tickets booked, a new
life already mapped out. I watched as you spoke with
such certainty, your voice steady even though I could see
the cracks in your composure, the hurt you tried so hard
to bury.

I was numb. My mind went blank, every rational thought
drowned out by a rush of disbelief and pain. I felt
paralyzed, unable to process the magnitude of what you
were saying. In that moment, all I could do was nod, as if
agreeing would somehow ease the ache in my chest. But
inside, I was spiraling, every ounce of strength I had
crumbling under the weight of losing you.

You had always been my rock, my safe space. And now, I was losing you piece by piece, unable to do anything to stop it. I wanted to scream, to beg you to stay, to promise that we could work it out. But my brain told me to let you go, that maybe this was what you needed, what you deserved. Maybe someone else could give you the happiness I had failed to provide. Maybe someone else could love you better, see you better, be everything I couldn't.

You were already packing for your trip to the new city, ready to hunt for a fresh start, a new place to call home. You wore a brave face, one that said you were fine, that you were doing what needed to be done. But I saw the flicker of doubt in your eyes, the silent plea for me to fight for us, to not let go so easily. But I didn't. I stayed silent, trapped in my own insecurities and fears. I convinced myself it was for your best — that maybe you were right, maybe this was the path that would lead to your happiness.

I stood there, helpless, watching you slip away, knowing I was making the biggest mistake of my life. A mistake that would haunt me forever, creating a void nothing else could fill. I believed I was doing the right thing, but deep down, I knew I was letting go of the best thing that had ever happened to me. I failed you when it mattered most. I let my fear and doubts dictate my actions, and in doing so, I lost the one person who truly felt like home.

The Final Goodbye

Your new home in another city was ready, the movers were scheduled, and the date of your departure was set — just two days after my birthday. Your bags were packed, each filled with pieces of our shared memories, and your heart seemed just as heavy. You had made it clear that you wanted to stay for my birthday, to give us one last celebration together, a quiet testament to how much I still meant to you, even in the midst of our separation. We were both tiptoeing on the edge of our emotions, holding back what felt like a flood that could drown us at any moment.

My birthday was a simple affair this time, a far cry from the grand celebrations of the past. It was just a small gathering with my office friends, a muted attempt at festivity overshadowed by the looming finality of your departure. I could feel the weight of the day pressing down on us, each hour ticking by like the countdown to an ending we couldn't avoid. Your flight was set for early the next morning, and as the evening wore on, we packed your luggage together, our hands moving on autopilot while our minds reeled with the unspoken.

The moment came. Your flight was just hours away, and it was time to say our final goodbye. In the past, I would always carry your bags down, place them in the cab, and stand there watching until your car disappeared from my sight. But this time was different. I couldn't bring myself to go down with you, and you didn't ask me to. We both knew that we were on the brink of breaking down, and neither of us wanted to fall apart in front of the other.

The elevator arrived, and the doors opened with a soft ding. You turned back for one last glance, your eyes holding a mix of sadness, determination, and something that felt like a silent plea. As soon as the doors closed behind you, I felt the last fragile thread holding me together snap. I broke down, the tears pouring out uncontrollably, like a dam that had finally burst after years of holding back. I was sobbing, howling, crying like a wounded animal, unable to contain the pain that had been building inside me for so long. The crying didn't stop for hours; it felt endless, like a storm that would never pass.

As I sat there, drowning in my sorrow, a message from you flashed on my phone: "It's okay if we cannot build a life together. I will always be cheering for you from the sidelines." Your words felt like a final nail in the coffin, a gentle but definitive closure that I wasn't ready to accept. My whole being was screaming to call you back, to beg you to stay, to fight for what we had. But you were already gone, slipping out of my life for what felt like forever.

It was my mistakes, my immaturity, or my failure to understand what you truly needed. Whatever it was, it had pushed you so far away that I couldn't reach you anymore. Even if I screamed until my voice broke, I knew you wouldn't hear me. I had lost you — lost us — lost everything that we had built together, and the realization was like a punch to the gut that left me breathless. I had lost you forever, and no amount of tears could ever bring you back.

Shattered Dreams

After you left, I thought I understood what I was feeling, but nothing prepared me for the torrent of emotions that followed. The tears wouldn't stop, no matter how many times I washed my face or tried to compose myself. It was as if my grief had a mind of its own, pouring out uncontrollably, unrelenting. But more than my own pain, what haunted me was the thought of what you were going through. I could picture you crying, battling the same storm I was facing. The weight of it all was crushing, and I felt an overwhelming urge to punish myself for causing you so much pain. I was in utter despair, consumed by the horror of what I had put you through.

From the day you left, nothing felt the same. Everything around me and inside me changed, as if a part of my very soul had been ripped away. I didn't recognize myself anymore. I cried and missed you every single day, every single moment. The urge to call you, to beg you to come back, was overwhelming. But I felt paralyzed, consumed by guilt and a sense of failure. I was convinced that I had let you down, that my cowardice had cost us everything. The confidence I once had was gone, replaced by a crushing sense of inadequacy. I lost the power to fight, the courage to be the person you needed me to be.

We still kept in touch, exchanging brief messages over chat, like distant echoes of what we once had. You in a different city, and I in another, it felt as though I had destroyed my own home and burned it to ashes. But in my heart, I was determined to rebuild everything between us. I knew I needed to get better, to be better, and I started working on myself quietly, without telling anyone. I had a plan in my mind — I would propose to you on your birthday, make it official, and give you the life you always dreamed of. I mapped out every detail, the exact date, the exact moment, the entire event playing out perfectly in my head.

I envisioned giving you everything you had ever wanted, the grand gesture you deserved, and in my mind, I clung to this hope like a lifeline. But before I could put my plan into action, you called me one day. I was driving when your name flashed on my screen, and I picked up, not knowing that everything was about to change. Your voice was steady, but there was an unfamiliar distance in your tone. You told me you were seeing someone new, that it was still in the early stages, but you wanted me to know. And then, you asked me not to call or text you anymore.

I could feel my heart shatter in that moment. I was driving, but suddenly the road blurred, and I pulled over to the side, parking the car in a quiet corner. As you spoke, all the plans I had made in my head, all the dreams of getting us back, crumbled right before my eyes. I realized, painfully, that I had been too late. I had wasted too much time, waiting for the perfect moment that never came. I listened in silence, unable to find the words to fight for us. When you hung up, it felt like you had disconnected from my life entirely.

I sat there in the car, my mind spinning, unable to process the words I had just heard. My chest felt tight, each breath a struggle as if the air had been knocked out of me. The world outside the windshield blurred and distorted, but inside, all I could feel was a suffocating emptiness that threatened to swallow me whole. My hands gripped the steering wheel so tightly that my knuckles turned white, as if holding on to it could somehow anchor me back to reality. But nothing made sense. Nothing felt real. All I could hear was your voice echoing in my head, the words that tore through every fragile thread of hope I had left.

I broke down, unable to hold it in any longer. The sobs came in violent waves, shaking my entire body as I screamed into the emptiness of the car. The sound of my own voice, raw and guttural, filled the space but offered no comfort. It was a sound of pure anguish, a desperate cry that no one would hear. I punched the dashboard, over and over, the pain in my knuckles a mere whisper compared to the agony inside my chest. Tears streamed down my face, hot and relentless, blurring my vision as if trying to drown out the reality I couldn't face.

I couldn't stop thinking about how I had let it all slip through my fingers, how I had been so close to reaching out, to making things right, and yet I hesitated. And now, it was too late. You were moving on, and I was left behind, stranded in a sea of regret and self-loathing. I felt like I was imploding, my heart caving in under the weight of everything I had lost. My mind raced with questions that had no answers — what if I had just called sooner? What if I had fought harder, been braver, told you how much you meant to me before it was too late?

The pain was unbearable, an all-consuming fire that burned away every shred of hope and left nothing but ashes. I wanted to scream until my throat gave out, to cry until there were no tears left. I felt completely and utterly broken, my dreams reduced to dust, my plans for our future lying in ruins. The life I had envisioned for us, the moments I had replayed in my head a thousand times, all crumbled in an instant. And as I sat there, shaking and sobbing, I knew that no amount of tears could ever bring back what was lost.

There was an emptiness inside me, a gaping void where my heart used to be, and I didn't know how to fill it. All I could feel was the relentless ache of what could have been, the bitter taste of regret that lingered on my tongue. I was drowning in it, suffocating under the weight of my own mistakes, and for the first time, I truly understood what it meant to be utterly alone. I wished I could turn back time, rewrite the ending that was unfolding before me, but I was powerless — trapped in a reality where the love of my life was slipping further and further away, and all I could do was watch.

I realized in that moment that I had lost you forever. And all the regret in the world couldn't change that.

Echoes of Yesterday

Not a single day has passed without the haunting presence of your thoughts. Each morning, I wake to the cold, unrelenting reality of your absence, and every night, my pillows bear the weight of my sorrow, drenched with tears that refuse to be dried. My life, once vibrant and filled with promise, has spiraled into a dark abyss of depression. I've been fighting this battle alone, silent and solitary, unable to share the depths of my despair with anyone.

My struggle isn't just for me; it's for my aging parents who depend on me, who have placed their hopes and trust in me to take care of everything around them. I've had to rise from the ashes like a phoenix, not for my own sake, but for theirs. Every day, I put on a mask — a facade of normalcy and strength — hiding the anguish that festers beneath. It's a cruel, unending charade, and the weight of this mask is growing heavier by the day.

The friends who once embraced me as one of their own have begun to distance themselves, their sympathy turning into a quiet judgment. I feel like a pariah, abandoned in the midst of my suffering. They urged me to move on, to leave the house that was once our sanctuary, the place where we dreamed and built a future together. But how can I abandon a place so saturated with your essence?

This house, our home, has become a shrine to our memories. Every corner still holds the echoes of your laughter, every room carries the imprint of your presence. I've preserved it just as you liked it—down to the last detail. I follow the routine you established, cleaning and decorating in the way you preferred, trying desperately to keep the remnants of you alive in this empty space.

Each time I walk through these rooms, the silence is punctuated by ghostly echoes of our past. I can almost hear you calling my name, "Nana," reverberating through the walls like a distant memory I can't quite grasp. The sound is both comforting and agonizing, a reminder of the life we once shared. I catch fleeting glimpses of your essence in the corners of my vision, shadows of you darting just beyond my reach. I imagine you running and hiding, a playful specter of what once was, a cruel trick of the mind that mocks me with what could have been.

The house stands as a monument to our life together, meticulously maintained as a shrine to our love. Every detail—every picture, every piece of furniture, every decoration—has been preserved just as you left it. It's my desperate attempt to keep you alive, to hold on to the fragments of our shared existence. I cling to the hope that someday, somehow, you will walk through that door and tell me it was all just a dream—a nightmare I can finally wake from. The anticipation of that impossible moment is both a balm and a torment, a promise of a future that will never come.

In the quiet solitude of the night, I still sleep in the same corner of the bed we once shared. The empty space beside me feels like a chasm, a void that no amount of tears or longing can fill. I keep my gaze fixed on that vacant spot, praying for a miracle, for the chance to see you lying there again, to feel your warmth beside me. Each morning, I wake to the harsh reality of your absence, the dream of your return shattered by the cold light of day. This house, this life, is a constant reminder of what we had and what I have lost. It is both a sanctuary and a prison—a place where your memory lives on and where my heart remains forever captive to the past.

Every corner of this home is infused with the essence of you. The walls echo with laughter that will never return, and the rooms are filled with the silent whispers of memories too precious to forget. I move through these spaces with a sense of melancholy, each step a reminder of the void left behind. The house, once a symbol of our love and future, now stands as a bittersweet testament to what we once had and can never regain. I am trapped in a relentless cycle of remembrance and regret, my heart aching for the days when you were here and my soul mourning the life we lost.

Lessons of Love

In the aftermath of our time together, the lessons you imparted linger in the quiet spaces of my heart, each one a testament to the depth of your understanding and compassion. Your departure, while painful, revealed truths about love that I had never fully grasped before.

You taught me that loving someone doesn't mean holding on to them at all costs. You showed me that love can be expressed in letting go, in allowing someone to follow their own path even when it diverges from ours. This profound lesson reshaped my understanding of what it means to truly love someone. Your absence became a powerful reminder of the strength found in selfless acts of love, even when it means stepping away.

Even with all my flaws, my imperfections, and the mess I was back then, you made me feel lovable. You saw past my mistakes, my uncertainties, and my broken pieces. You loved me not in spite of them, but because of the person I was, deeply flawed yet wholly human. This acceptance was a gift I hadn't known I needed, a reflection of the love you gave that saw me for who I truly was.

You are one of the kindest, purest souls I have ever met. Your kindness was not a mere quality but a strength, a testament to your character that inspired me to see compassion in a new light. In a world that often feels harsh and unforgiving, you taught me that kindness is a superpower. It is a strength that can mend broken hearts and soothe the aching souls of those around us.

Your lesson on compassion went beyond mere words. You taught me to extend understanding to those who hurt us, to recognize that the ones who are hardest to love often need it the most. This realization was a balm to my wounded heart, a reminder that love can heal even the deepest of wounds. It's in those moments of greatest pain that love's true power reveals itself, showing us how to forgive and how to move forward with an open heart.

Through all the heartache and shattered dreams, you taught me that love is never wasted. Even when our hearts are broken into a billion pieces, love endures. It remains a force that allows us to understand and to empathize, to piece ourselves back together with the fragments of what once was. This enduring love, even in the face of pain, is a testament to its power and its capacity to transform.

Now, more than ever, I understand that your decision to walk away was, paradoxically, the greatest act of love you could perform. It was a sacrifice born of deep care and self-awareness, a choice made not out of cruelty but out of a profound understanding of what was best for both of us. In your leaving, you gave me the greatest gift of all: the chance to learn, to grow, and to discover the true meaning of love.

Fragments of a Lost Self

I never liked drinking. It was always something I avoided, a vice that seemed foreign and distasteful. But now, as if by some cruel twist of fate, I can't imagine a day without it. Each glass is a temporary escape, a numbing agent for the pain that has taken over my soul.

I never liked nicotine. The smell, the habit, the way it clung to the air and to the soul — it was always something I detested. Yet now, here I am, an addict, my fingers stained and my breath tainted. The cigarettes are a crutch, a way to dull the edges of my existence.

I never liked late nights. The silence of the darkness always unsettled me, and the hours seemed to stretch endlessly. But now, I find myself conversing with the owls, my nocturnal companions. The night has become my refuge, and the owls my only listeners in the solitude of the dark.

I never lost days to my demons. I was always strong, always resilient. But now, I've begun to lose months, each one slipping through my fingers like grains of sand. The demons have grown stronger, their grip tighter, and I find myself drowning in a sea of despair.

I never shed a tear out of fear. Tears were something I avoided, a sign of weakness I couldn't afford. But now, every tear is a manifestation of my fears, a testament to the shattered pieces of my heart. I fear every drop, every sob, for they are a reflection of the anguish I can't escape.

I never skipped a beat. My life was a rhythmic dance, each step measured and purposeful. Now, I've lost my rhyme. The music has stopped, and I am left stumbling, trying to find my way in a world that no longer makes sense.

This road doesn't lead home. The familiar paths have twisted into unknown territory, and the world feels foreign, a labyrinth with no clear exit. The certainty I once had has been replaced by an overwhelming sense of dread.

I've lost the very essence of who I am. The person I once was has become a distant memory, spinning aimlessly like a stranded turtle, vulnerable and exposed. Vultures circle above, eyeing me as easy prey, sensing the weakness that now defines me.

Every day, I feel myself getting a little closer to losing my way completely. The darkness that once was a mere shadow has become my constant companion, and the road ahead seems more uncertain with each passing moment.

I am adrift in a sea of my own making, and as the days blur into one another, I wonder if I will ever find my way back to who I once was. The fragments of my lost self are scattered, and I am left to piece them together in a world that no longer feels like home.

The Unspoken Truth

In the quiet moments of solitude, I find myself wrestling with thoughts I can barely articulate. The yearning to reach out, to bridge the chasm that separates us, is a constant ache in my heart. I really want to talk to you. The words are on the tip of my tongue, but I'm paralyzed by the fear of sounding annoying. I don't want to intrude on your life or add to your burdens. Yet, every day feels incomplete without hearing your voice, without sharing the mundane and the extraordinary moments that used to fill our conversations.

I really want to tell you how much I miss you. The emptiness in my days is a stark reminder of your absence. But how can I express this without sounding needy? I don't want to be a source of discomfort or make you feel obligated to respond. The void you left behind is vast and profound, and every attempt to convey my feelings seems to fall short, overshadowed by the fear of overstepping boundaries.

I really want to say how much I love you. The depth of my affection is something I carry with me every day, a silent testament to what we shared. But how can I tell you this without feeling desperate? My heart aches to communicate the intensity of my feelings, yet I am paralyzed by the fear of appearing as though I am clinging to a past that has moved on.

I really want to tell you how sad I have been lately. The weight of my sorrow is a constant companion, and the burden feels too heavy to carry alone. But how do I share this without feeling dumb? I don't want to be a burden or to sound as if I am seeking sympathy. My sadness is a private anguish, and the thought of revealing it makes me feel vulnerable and exposed.

I really want to tell you how many times I have pretended to be happy. The façade of normalcy has become a mask I wear to shield myself from the rawness of my emotions. But how do I confess this without feeling fake? The dissonance between my outward appearance and inner turmoil is a painful reminder of what I have lost, and the thought of admitting this feels like a betrayal of the strength I've tried so hard to project.

I really want to have a regular conversation with you. The desire to reconnect, to share in the everyday exchanges that once brought us closer, is a longing that consumes me. But how do I initiate this without revealing the depth of my feelings? I want to engage in casual dialogue, yet every word feels like a window into the depths of my heart, exposing the raw vulnerability I have worked so hard to conceal.

Each attempt to bridge the gap between us feels like a balancing act, a tightrope walk over the chasm of uncertainty. The unspoken truth of my emotions lingers, a silent cry for understanding that I struggle to voice. I am caught between the desire to reach out and the fear of the response, navigating a labyrinth of my own making where every step is fraught with the tension of the unknown.

In this delicate dance of words and emotions, I am left to wonder if there will ever be a way to bridge the silence, to share the truth of my heart without the weight of judgment or the fear of being misunderstood. The longing for connection is a bittersweet symphony, and the notes of my unspoken truth echo in the empty spaces where your presence once filled.

Echoes of a Love Unfulfilled

In the quiet moments of reflection, I am haunted by the echoes of what could have been. Regret seeps into the corners of my thoughts, a constant reminder of choices made and paths not taken. I wish I had handled things differently. I wish we both had. The what-ifs and could-have-beens swirl around me like a storm I cannot escape. Yet, amidst the storm, there is a clear and unwavering truth: I do not regret loving you.

Even if our time together was fleeting, even if we were only a beautiful, transient moment in each other's lives, my love for you persists. Even now, with you gone, my heart holds on to that love with a fierce, undying grip. It's a love that defies the constraints of time and space, a love that proves its reality through the pain it endures. The ache of your absence is a testament to the depth of my feelings. It hurts, yet it does not deter me. You are no longer mine, but I will always belong to you.

In the realms of my dreams and wishes, I find solace in the hope of another lifetime. In that alternate reality, I hope we get the chance to love each other again, without the shadow of heartache that clouds our present. I dream of a time when our love can flourish without the pain that marks our current existence.

I imagine a lifetime where we share the bedsheets, where our bodies intertwine as we drift off to sleep. I envision mornings beginning with the warmth of your embrace and evenings ending with your laughter echoing through the room. In this alternate life, our nights are filled with joy, not just in dreams but in reality, as we dance and laugh together in the kitchen, creating memories that defy the constraints of time.

In this imagined future, a simple hug from you starts my day and another ends it. Your presence becomes a comforting constant, a source of daily happiness that I have longed for and missed. As the Earth continues its eternal rotation, I hope that you, too, will turn around and find your way back to me.

This longing for another chance, for a different outcome, is a bittersweet solace I cling to. It is a hope that the love we shared, no matter how temporary, might find its way back to us in another lifetime. Until then, I remain here, holding on to the echoes of a love unfulfilled, dreaming of the day when we might find each other again.

The Silence of a Shattered Heart

I didn't fall in love with you out of need, or because I yearned for someone to hold close. I didn't seek you out to fill a void or to make me feel loved. My love for you wasn't born out of desperation or loneliness. It was something far deeper, something that happened in an instant and took me by complete surprise.

The moment I met you, the world around us seemed to pause. The clamor of life faded into silence, and the sounds that once filled the air were suddenly muted. All that remained was the purity of your voice, cutting through the stillness like a beacon. Each time I looked into your eyes, I felt a profound sense of belonging, as if I had finally found my home.

In those moments, my only thought was how to make you happy, to ensure that your life was filled with joy and love. You were doing so much for me, more than you even realized, and I wanted nothing more than to return that kindness a thousandfold. I wanted to be the one to support you, to stand by your side, and to cherish every second we spent together.

But as time went on, the inevitable began to unfold. You started to drift away, slowly and quietly, like a ship setting sail into an ever-expanding sea. It was the cruelest realization, knowing that there was nothing I could do to prevent it, nothing that could anchor you to me. You were slipping away, and I was powerless to stop it.

The pain of watching you leave was a heavy, suffocating weight, a torment that I felt in every fiber of my being. Even as you departed, leaving a void where once there was warmth, you carved out a place in my heart that would forever remain yours. Whether I wanted it or not, a part of me was irrevocably yours.

I have never experienced love like that before, a love so intense and consuming that it etched itself into the very core of my soul. Even though it ended up breaking my heart, the love we shared was unlike anything I had known. It was a rare and beautiful flame that, despite its fleeting nature, left a lasting imprint on my life.

In the silence of my heart, where echoes of our time together linger, I am left with the bittersweet reality of a love that once was. It was a love that made me feel whole, that brought me home, and even in its absence, it remains a part of who I am. The silence may have followed your departure, but the memories and the love continue to resonate, a testament to a connection that transcends the pain of its ending.

The Last Message

This book is dedicated to just one person—my way of apologizing, of reaching out across the distance that now separates us, in the hope that somehow, this message will reach you before your birthday ends. Loving you was unfamiliar, like navigating uncharted waters, but it was also the most comforting experience of my life. I have never loved anyone else like this before, and I don't think I ever will again.

I am grateful for the time we spent together, the memories we created, and the moments that made me feel alive. Thank you for making me feel good about being me, for always asking if I was okay, and for the countless times you told me you were proud of me. Those words meant more than you will ever know, and they still echo in my mind, a reminder of the kindness you showed me when I needed it most.

It's sad, isn't it? That we never fulfilled our lifetime commitment. Those promises we made, the ones that were supposed to carry us through all of life's challenges—they haunt me now, a constant reminder of what could have been. But even with the weight of regret, I don't regret falling for you. I will forever cherish this feeling, the stories you told, and the laughter we shared. They are etched into my soul, memories that I cling to even as time tries to wash them away.

I know you love me—I felt it in every touch, every word, every look. But I also know that you are seeing someone else now, and that knowledge cuts deep. Yet, even as you are in the arms of another, my love for you remains unwavering. I won't be there beside you, but I will always be here for you, silently cheering you on from the sidelines. Ignoring you will be a daily struggle, a quiet torment, but it's the only way I know how to set you free.

This book is my way of keeping our story alive, of immortalizing our love even if we are no longer together. It serves as a testament to what we once shared, a beacon that preserves the essence of our bond. Through its pages, I hope to capture the beauty of our love, to remind us both that, despite the distance and the silence, the affection we nurtured will continue to bloom. Each word, each memory, is a fragment of a love that transcends the barriers of time and space.

I guess this is also my farewell message.
There's so much I want to say, so much I want
to express, but words feel inadequate to
convey the depth of my feelings. I've spent
countless days and sleepless nights writing
this memento for you, pouring every ounce of
my heart into these pages. It wasn't easy to
retrace our steps, to relive those moments that
once filled me with joy but now bring a
bittersweet ache. With every word I wrote, I
shed tears — tears of longing, of sorrow, of love
that hasn't faded with time.

Journeying down memory lane was like
navigating a minefield; every step threatened
to break me. My heart felt heavy, the memories
pressing down like a weight I couldn't lift.
There were times when I found it hard to
breathe, when the sorrow was so
overwhelming that it stole the air from my
lungs. I know there are things I've missed,
pieces of our story that I couldn't bear to put
into words. But writing this journal has been
the hardest thing I've ever done.

Each word is a piece of me, a fragment of the
love I still carry. And though this may be the
last gift I can give you, know that it comes
from the deepest parts of my soul. I hope that,
wherever life takes you, these words will
remind you of a love that was real, a love that,
despite everything, still beats within me.

This is my final message, my quiet goodbye. I hope it reaches you, and I hope it brings you some semblance of the comfort you once gave me. May this book serve as a bridge across the distance, a symbol of a love that endures beyond our separation, forever preserved in its pages.